CONTENTS

FOREWORD

Trends towards increased censorship, and a culture encouraging self-censorship, within contemporary fine art and higher education, have increased significantly in recent times.

This publication is a dossier with contextual information concerning censorship of art, and the official encouragement of self-censorship, on the Master of Fine Art Programme at Glasgow School of Art during 2017 and 2018. It is informed by extensive research and analysis, plus consultations with relevant specialists speaking off the record. It does not benefit from input by legal or investigative journalism specialists. Should the sequence of events at Glasgow School of Art come under further scrutiny this publication makes available some relevant materials. If it does not then this publication simply makes public these events in an accessible format. Some of the material is already in the public domain, but remains scattered. As the publication is largely a dossier of evidence, there is some repetition of information throughout.

While the circumstances are specific, the underlying issues are broad and perennial. A core principle involved is the relationship between the systematic application of control, and the power of creative enquiry & expression. In places dedicated to formation and development of people and fields of endeavour – such places including formal education – where horizons of possibility may open or byzantine entanglements proliferate, the stakes increase when paymasters and managers play usurper.

At the time of publication, May 2018, students on the Programme who are about to graduate do not know what direction the MFA Programme will take on the issue of censorship directives issued to the student body. The decision on whether the directives will be removed from the MFA Programme Handbook, as requested by a majority of current MFA students in a written petition, has been deferred until after their graduation.

- Om Lekha, May 2018

1

TIMELINE

April – May 2017 Scrutiny of proposed MFA student James Oberhelm art installation "Effects" *[The Enthronement]* by Senior Management Team at Glasgow School of Art, and censorship of the work from public exhibition from the MFA Interim Show, due to video content in the work.

May – June 2017 Requests by student for written explanation of censorship decision ignored by GSA, and following Freedom of Information request by Nik Williams of free-speech advocacy group Scottish PEN responded to evasively. Request by Mr. Williams for a full internal review of the decision as required under Freedom of Information legislation. Internal documents publicly released June 2017.

May – Aug 2017 Consultations and correspondence between student and staff members at GSA Student Representative Council, resulting in meeting of SRC Director Laura Glennie with GSA Deputy Director (Academic) Prof. Ken Neil, and Head of School of Fine Art Dr. Alastair Payne, to discuss censorship decision in April. Minutes of meeting supplied to student by Laura Glennie.

Sept 2017 Incoming MFA student yeargroup briefed by MFA Programme Leader Henry Rogers at official MFA Programme Induction, and warned that unacceptable artworks will not be permitted for exhibition at GSA.

Oct 2017 Report on censorship of *"Effects" [The Enthronement]* sent to Brussels-based Artists Rights Justice Working Group by Nik Williams, for their annual report, and supply to the United Nations Special Rapporteur on cultural rights.

Nov 2017 All MFA students sent a new MFA Programme Handbook, stating broad categories under which artwork produced by students deemed unacceptable will be censored at GSA.

Nov 2017 – Feb 2018 Meetings and correspondence resulting from Handbook censorship section, resulting in a student petition calling for removal of the section sent to MFA Programme Leader, and supplied to all MFA staff. Response stating that it will be given due consideration at a staff meeting within 3 weeks.

March 2018 Email sent to students by MFA Programme Leader stating that the decision on the petition will be made during summer 2018

May 2017 – May 2018 Media coverage of events at GSA by Index on Censorship, and other reportage.

SECTION I: CURRENT & ONGOING CENSORSHIP PHASE

A. Written censorship directives to all MFA students, November 2017

The 'MFA Programme Handbook', sent to students on 2nd November 2017, contains the section 'ethical good practice' which warns of the limits to acceptable artistic production by students on the MFA Programme. The following is the petition sent by MFA students to the MFA Programme Leader. The petition was signed by 34 students on the Programme, of a total 50 students enrolled.

[Text in bold is from the MFA Programme Handbook]

Letter to MFA Course leader regarding the proposed MFA Handbook:

We, the undersigned students write to you to call for the following sections -to be removed from the proposed MFA handbook.

In the section **"WHAT WE ARE COMMITTED TO"**

• the production of work that adheres to the 'highest ethical standards' and 'ethical good practice'.

In the section **"ALL THAT WE DO IS PREDICATED ON"**

• inculcating your knowledge and understanding of ethical good practice, your ethical responsibilities to others and the sensitivities of other people and your ethical responsibilities in the public presentation of work in whatever form it may take;

• extending this ethical good practice and your ethical responsibilities not only to people, but also to non-human subjects (animals) and the planet as an interdependent ecological system in all of its tragic splendour;

• our understanding of our rights and our responsibilities within the context of the Glasgow School of Art and in relationship to Scottish, UK, EU and International laws;

• our understanding that our right to freedom of speech is not absolute, we cannot do and say whatever we like because it may be against the law e.g. hate speech;

• our understanding that material classed as 'offensive' or 'inappropriate material' may actually be illegal and therefore the Ethics Committee will not approve its usage;

• our understanding that culling material from the internet breeches copyright law as the material is not always free to use;

• our understanding that whilst we may enjoy all that the Glasgow School of Art can offer us and we have the right of access to its facilities, in joining any programme that GSA offers we also have obligations to the institution, by NOT bringing the institution into disrepute.

Examples of our reasons for calling for the removal of the above listed sections are set out below, and are not limited to these examples:

The above sections seem more concerned with curating an MFA brand of artworks than in fostering critical thinking within the student body.

"culling material from the internet breeches copyright law" - Generating all your own visual imagery and collaging existing material are two distinct art practices and it would be ridiculous to not be allowed to do the latter.

The Situationists techniques of appropriation, collaging & detournment of existing imagery has been a distinct art practice since the 60's, what is being proposed in the handbook seems a marked step backwards in art.

<u>Censorship is fundamentally a point of principle, even if it doesn't affect an individual practice right now. We believe the following will be affected to a detrimental and unacceptable degree:</u>

Working in an environment where artistic integrity is supported, rather than monitored for perceived offensiveness, inappropriateness, being disreputable etc.

Working free from the threat of being banned by GSA.

Wanting to work in an environment where the artistic process is respected and supported in its own terms, not downgraded and made subject to other agendas, such as those posed under the term 'ethics', which can be interpreted in many ways.

Wanting to work in an environment where the 'chilling-effect' on the production of artwork is absent, due to the explicit threat of added bureaucracy, and possibly being banned, i.e. wanting to work in an environment where self-censorship is not encouraged.

The necessity to work in an environment where the transformative potential of art-practice is understood, so that potentially difficult subjects and materials can be addressed through our art, e.g. work dealing with sexuality, death, the sacred, sociopolitical conflict.

Wanting a relationship of respect towards our art practice and ourselves, rather than a relationship where students are told to accept values imposed upon them, or 'inculcated' into such values.

Wanting to work in an environment where creativity is valued by staff and students alike, not denigrated by tactics of contractual and managerial coercion

The value of supporting an environment where the greatest potential creative development is made possible for each of us, for our fellow students, and us collectively, and for future students. Thus to support the integrity of the course itself, and the integrity of art practice more broadly as a distinct and important endeavour.

B. Verbal censorship directive to Year 1 student group, September 2017

At the official induction onto the MFA Programme on 14th September 2017, the incoming student yeargroup for 2017-19 were briefed by the MFA Programme Leader on a wide range of issues concerning the Programme, including their being warned about artistic content. No single definitive account exists on this briefing, due to students attending wishing to remain off the record. Accounts given indicate that the MFA Programme Leader briefed students about the limits on work they may produce according to general criteria, and citing the specific example of artwork using 'terrorist materials'.

SECTION II: CONTEXTUAL OP-ED

Developments at Glasgow School of Art regarding censorship of art and the curtailing of free-speech and open expression are not happening in isolation, but are part of prevailing and emergent trends. The issues are live and ongoing, and have generated a large amount of analysis, and comment. Despite this there is a tendency among many to go along with emergent policies and practices that curtail open expression without sufficient analysis of the implications. Censorship is particularly insidious because it deprives enquiring minds access to the very materials that sharpen analysis and discernment – to information, to the way information is communicated, and to the who, why, & how of communicative relationships. By its nature censorship is infantilizing to those denied access. This has consequences. All political decisions and acts involve risks of inviting unforeseen consequences; when the political decision, censorship, involves denying people the ability to see even what's going on around them, it spells trouble.

Nick Cohen, author of *You Can't Read This Book: Censorship in an Age of Freedom*, is a writer and journalist who has analysed and critiqued these political trends for many years. The following article was first published in The Observer on 13th January 2018. It is available online at

https://www.theguardian.com/commentisfree/2018/jan/13/censorship-wins-no-arguments-and-just-helps-the-right

<u>Censorship wins no arguments and just helps the right</u>

Nick Cohen

How you think is as important as what you think. If you believe you can ban your way to victory by mounting heresy hunts against all who veer from the true faith, you will not only deserve to lose by some airy moral reckoning. You will lose whether you deserve to or not. As losing is no longer a trivial event in the age of Brexit and Trump, it is worth understanding the consequences of going beyond the old liberal principle that only demagogues who incite violence should be banned.

The moral arguments against censorship are so old I can recite them in my sleep. The practical case against a "liberal" movement that reaches for the censor's red pen like a drunk reaching for a bottle deserves more attention.

People who call themselves progressives don't worry enough about unintended consequences because they lack the broadness of mind to see themselves as others see them. They see no reason to treasure free debate. No argument will persuade Donald Trump or Nigel Farage to hold up their hands and admit they are wrong. Their dedicated supporters, meanwhile, are no more likely to change their minds than fanatical believers in any other political ideology or religious creed. These are good points that are beside the point, because they are based on a deep ignorance of how debates work.

You don't argue to convert your opponents. You argue to persuade the undecided audience watching on in silence, as it judges which side is worthy of support. I doubt that waverers nod their heads in approval when universities, of all places, do not allow speakers to appear on platforms, or when the state capitalists of Virgin Rail refuse to stock the *Daily Mail*. Look at them, and maybe look at yourself too. It's not a compelling sight.

For all their bombast, censors give every appearance of being dictatorial neurotics, who are so frightened of their opponents that they cannot find the strength to take them on in the open. I can't imagine many saying, "I'll side with the people who tell me what I can and can't think." I find it equally hard to picture readers turning away from the Mail because Sir Richard Branson and "alternative" comedians who haven't had an alternative thought since Blair's second term tell them to.

"Liberals" still do not understand that when they censor they are falling into their enemy's trap. The alt-right is as much a satirical as a political movement: more South Park than The West Wing. It is at its happiest trolling liberal culture rather than governing, which is why Brexit and the Trump administration are so shambolic. The alt-right wants to and needs to provoke liberals into showing they are repressive, so it cast itself in the role of transgressive rebel. Why play the part it has allotted you?

We are in a contradictory culture. On the one hand, "liberals" rightly say that sexists, racists and homophobes are preposterous bigots. On the other, they run away from the chance to confront them. If you can't beat a bigot in argument, you shouldn't ban them but step aside and make way for people who can. It's not as if they have impressive cases that stand up to scrutiny.

As pertinently for those wondering how a pornographic thug like Trump or such transparent charlatans as Johnson and Farage can win, if you don't debate them, you will never learn how to defeat them. You won't feel the ripple in the audience as you make a good case or telling jibe. You won't learn which shots hit home and which miss the mark. When the battle is finally joined, you will enter it unarmed, then look around in bewilderment when you are defeated.

In the hours after Trump's victory, the American author Walter Mosley said Democrats had put on "the blinders of superiority" when they assumed he must surely lose. There is no more effective way for the superior to blind themselves to the world around them than by refusing to argue with it.

Again, I am not making a moral point – we can save John Milton and George Orwell for another day. As a matter of practical politics, you had better be very sure that you will win before pandering to inquisitorial desires. So much of what passes for "liberal" debate just assumes that liberals have already won and possess the power to decide what is read and said. They don't fret that reactionaries in office will use the arguments in favour of censorship that liberals have nurtured to restrict their freedom to speak. Nor do they question whether their repression will work.

Harvard's Stephen Pinker recently listed true but "politically incorrect" assertions that have driven American students rightwards when they discovered US campuses rarely discuss them. His unpalatable propositions included: capitalism is preferable to communism – no one would prefer to live in North rather than South Korea, after all; most of the world's suicide terrorists are Islamists; and different ethnic groups commit violent crime at different rates.

Pinker said that if only universities had the courage to face awkward facts they could make perfectly good rejoinders against the apparent justifications for racism and anarcho-capitalism. The most successful capitalist societies have strong welfare states rather than unregulated markets, for instance. Most American terrorists are white supremacists. Ethnicity isn't destiny and the propensity of a group to commit crimes changes over time.

Inevitably, creepy American leftists cut his explanation out when they edited a video of his talk to present him as a fascist. They should have thought harder about the failure of US campuses to impose their taboos in a setting where liberals have power. It is a warning that authoritarian liberalism is an impossible project. Let's try a thought experiment. Even if you were to suppress the rightwing press and rightwing social media, as so many "liberals" appear to want to do, you would not ban rightwing ideas, merely win them more converts by investing them with a dissident glamour. What's next? Vet candidates for office to make sure they conform to your desires? Stop your opponents voting?

The motivation behind much modern censorship is essentially religious: an affirmation of the urge to parade your righteousness. It is an egocentric and frivolous emotion to indulge at a time when the stakes could not be higher, and every opponent of the populist status quo ought to be concentrating on winning converts rather than driving them into the arms of their grateful opponents.

SECTION III: INITIAL CENSORSHIP PHASE

In April-May 2017 Glasgow School of Art banned the proposed installation *"Effects" [The Enthronement]* from the MFA Interim Show, the first time a student artwork had been censored from public exhibition on the MFA Programme. The censorship warning to MFA students in September 2017 [see Section I, B.] made explicit mention of prohibitions on use of 'terrorist materials', thus showing a development from what was potentially the one-off censorship of a single work, to a policy platform on the Programme designed to instill all students with an ethos of self-censorship, by directing them away from work with difficult materials. Crucially, the later directives are of a general, 'catch-all', nature with regards to perceived transgression and dissidence. This section collects the documents generated specifically in relation to the earlier censoring of *"Effects" [The Enthronement]*.

A. Press Release, issued May 2017

PRESS RELEASE

<u>Regarding censorship of art by Glasgow School of Art, May 2017</u>

Glasgow School of Art has censored from exhibition an artwork proposed for exhibition by an MFA student, the first time in the history of the Masters course that this has happened.

The art installation was scheduled for exhibition in the Glasgow School of Art's 'Interim Show' in May. The installation deals with the geopolitics of the Middle East region over the past century, and the intimate impact of war due to bereavement. It presents the various forms of media and technology used during that time, by imperialist and fundamentalist organizations, and by bureaucracies trying to cope with the realities of casualties incurred by military service.

In representing the trajectory from the geopolitics of the 1914-18 war to the conflicts of today the installation includes two videos issued by Al-Hayat, the media outlet of Daesh/Isis, in 2014. The videos in question address the Sykes-Picot Agreement of 1916, out of which the current Iraq-Syria border was initially conceived. They are counterposed in the artwork by the 1916 map depicting the first proposed border. The decision to censor focuses on the inclusion of the contemporary videos, to the exclusion of all other aspects of the work.

In previous cases where artworks proposed for exhibition contained difficult or distressing content, this was addressed through a consultative process, and an appropriate management plan for exhibition of the artwork. Despite a similar process in this case the artwork has been censored on the grounds of 'inappropriate content'. As previous artworks have also included difficult material, yet gone ahead to exhibition, it suggests that the censorship of this piece has a political dimension. Thus the decision fails to account for the artistic employment and context of the videos, which locates them as part of the semiotics of control, intersecting with lived reality across the historical timespan.

The decision to censor appears to prioritize narrow political considerations over Glasgow School of Art's own duties and interests: supporting artists in their responsibility to engage with the visual culture of our times, and to participate in meaningful dialogue with the society they are part of.

B. Index on Censorship online articles

https://www.indexoncensorship.org/2017/05/glasgow-school-of-art-censorship-isis/

NEWS

Glasgow School of Art bans student's controversial artwork

12 May 2017
BY RYAN MCCHRYSTAL

The flyer for master's student James Oberhelm's banned artwork "Effects" [The Enthronement]

The internationally famous Glasgow School of Art has censored an artwork by one of its students in what is claimed to be the first time in the history of its master's course.

The work by fine art student James Oberhelm is not being shown in full, but visitors to the exhibition in the art college are told by a flier that the rest of the exhibit has been censored.

The college, whose famous alumni include Peter Capaldi, Liz Lochhead and Charles Rennie Mackintosh, says the ban was in place because of concerns about its "inappropriate content".

"Effects" [The Enthronement], which was scheduled for exhibition during the first day of Glasgow School of Art's Interim Show this month, deals with the geopolitics of the Middle East, specifically the century between the 1916 Sykes-Picot Agreement, in which between Britain and France redrew the map of the Middle East, and now.

It was to include a video monitor playing two propaganda videos issues by Isis in 2014: one, entitled The End of Sykes-Picot, shows the destruction of part of the border between Iraq and Syria following the organisation's capture of territories; the other, Kaser al Hudud, depicts bulldozers destroying the earthen wall along the same border.

A spokesperson for The Glasgow School of Art said: "We deemed the filmic material to be inappropriate for public display as we were concerned that the student's use and distribution of that material could present and unacceptable risk for the student and the GSA."

Oberhelm believes that this is the first time in the history of the Glasgow School of Art's master's course that such an instance of censorship has occurred, although a representative from the course was unavailable to confirm this. In another instance, a work was deemed too pornographic was granted a separate exhibition space with a disclaimer, Oberhelm said.

"The decision to censor appears to prioritise narrow political considerations over Glasgow School of Art's own duties and interests: supporting artists in their responsibility to engage with the visual culture of our times, and to participate in meaningful dialogue with the society they are part of," Oberhelm said in a press release.

A freedom of information request was made to the Glasgow School of Art, requesting: "all correspondence, information or documents held by the GSA regarding the decision to remove the piece…as well as the grounds for its removal." The school has guaranteed a response no later than 6 June.

the voice of free expression

NEWS

Turner Prize winner criticises Glasgow School of Art for censoring student's work

The explanation given to James Oberhelm for the removal of his work from an interim show was "inadequate" according to artist Duncan Campbell

24 May 2017
BY RYAN MCCHRYSTAL

Earlier this month Index on Censorship reported on the Glasgow School of Art's censoring of master of fine arts student James Oberhelm's work, which the school deemed to contain "inappropriate content". This was the first and only time a work of art has been censored in the history of the MFA course.

The work, "Effects" [The Enthronement], is an installation dealing with the geopolitics of the Middle East, specifically the centenary of the Sykes-Picot Agreement.

Duncan Campbell, the Irish Turner Prize winner and former student of the Glasgow School of Art, told Index: "In appropriating such demanding representations there is a difficult discussion about responsibility, accountability, and answerability to be had. If an MFA interim show isn't the place for this, I don't know where is."

The school disagrees. In response to a Freedom of Information request by Scottish Pen for "all correspondence, information or documents held by the GSA regarding the decision to remove the piece… as well as the grounds for its removal", the school said: "The [senior management team] decided that this particular film should not be shown and that the student be supported in moving forward in terms of professional practice and understanding the implications of their work including the presentation of online sources."

The film in question was a showreel of two videos issued by Al Hayat, Isis' media branch, in 2014, showing the dismantling of the border between Iraq and Syria as well as an execution sequence, which Oberhelm sourced from the public domain and included in the artwork.

Oberhelm maintains that the response to the FOI request represents a lack of transparency and told Index that his repeated requests to have the reasons for the decision to censor his work in writing, although promised, have been repeatedly denied.

On 11 April Oberhelm was informed via email that his work "is now going to be reviewed by the 'Prevent Concerns Group'".

The school's Prevent Concerns Group consists of 17 executive and non-executive members, made up of senior staff members including the director, the deputy director and the head of the school of fine art. It is "responsible for the strategic development and implementation of measures to meet the Prevent Duty".

The UK government's Prevent strategy for safeguarding communities against the threat of terrorism has been criticised by, among others, Index over concerns it undermines the value of freedom by feeding "the very commodity that the terrorists thrive on: fear."

During a chance encounter on the street with MFA course director Henry Rogers on 26 April, Oberhelm was given insufficient information on the reasons for the artwork's removal from the course's interim show. The encounter followed immediately after Rogers' meeting with Alistair Payne, the head of the school of fine art at the Glasgow School of Art, during which Rogers was informed of the decision about the installation's viability for exhibition. Rogers then informing Oberhelm that "the decision is no"

In the moments it took for the pair to walk to the JD Kelly building, a number of points were raised, including Prevent. No great amount of detail was given, but it was hinted that Prevent could be, although wasn't definitely, the basis for the decision.

Rogers also mentioned that an "ethics form" may have been necessary for the work to be shown, but he seemed unsure. "I informed him that I had not been told that an ethics form was required and that I had completed a risk assessment form," Oberhelm told Index.

The conversation ended with Oberhelm's request for a written statement explaining the terms under which the work had been censored, which Rogers said would have to be submitted in writing. Oberhelm's written request was then forwarded to Alistair Payne the following day. During another meeting between the two on 27 April, Oberhelm was told he would receive the minutes of the meeting during which the decision was made. As of yet, the school has not obliged with either any written explanation or the minutes, negating a basic requirement for institutional transparency.

Since Index published the news of the censoring of Oberhelm's work, the school hasn't provided us with any further information, despite our requests, and has not granted us an interview.

"[T]he initial FOI has been answered as have follow up questions and that the GSA has nothing to add to this," a spokesperson for the school told us.

Campbell told Index: "Given the highly consequential decision they have made, I find GSA's explanation for the removal of James Oberhelm's artwork inadequate. An honest statement of the committee's opinions and objections would have at least given everyone affected something to respond to. By being so wilfully non-committal they might as well have offered no explanation at all."

Campbell is one of many leading contemporary artists who has studied at the Glasgow School of Art and was the fifth artist who studied at the school, and the fourth artist to take part in the school's MFA programme, to win the prestigious Turner Prize.

When Campbell won in 2014, the director of the school, Tom Inns, said: "This is a great accolade both for Duncan and for The Glasgow School of Art … Duncan and all the previous GSA winners and shortlisted artists are a great inspiration to the current generation of students and the wider visual art community here in Glasgow."

But given that Campbell's Turner Prize-winning work, It For Others, contains an image of IRA volunteer Joe McCann, one has to wonder whether the work Inns offered "warm congratulations" for in 2014 would be censored by the school under Prevent if the artist was an MFA student today. After all, Northern Irish dissident republicans do still pose a threat of terrorism, including in Glasgow.

the voice of free expression

NEWS

Documents show Prevent used to censor Glasgow School of Art student's work

21 Jul 2017
BY CLAIRE KOPSKY

The flyer for master's student James Oberhelm's banned artwork "Effects" [The Enthronement]

After more than two months of waiting for a full response to a freedom of information request filed by Scottish Pen, the Glasgow School of Art has released a series of staff emails that explicitly show that Prevent, the UK's counter-terror program, was discussed in the process of the censoring of fine art student James Oberhelm's artwork.

"Prevent is supposed to safeguard communities against the threat of terrorism, but the strategy is, in effect, counterproductive," Melody Patry, Index on Censorship's head of advocacy said. "The government should be encouraging discussions about how to counter radicalisation, but, in this case, it has clearly silenced the artist's interrogation of extremism through his work."

Oberhelm's "Effects" [The Enthronement], which dealt with the geopolitics of the Middle East, was set to feature on the first day of the school's Interim Show in May. It included two propaganda videos issued by Isis, one of which showed an execution carried out by the extremist group on the border between Syria and Iraq. As the emails state, this is "difficult imagery".

Oberhelm acquired the films from the public domain and had planned for the work to feature several content warnings before showing the clips. An email from someone at GSA (the authors are redacted) on 10 April states: "I think this needs to be looked at by the Prevent Group." The email goes on to say that the artwork "needs to be considered by the Head of School and with his line manager."

Oberhelm says he was informed via email on 11 April that his work "is now going to be reviewed by the 'Prevent Concerns Group.'" The group is "responsible for the strategic development and implementation of measures to meet the Prevent Duty". His work was subsequently removed from the show.

Artist Bob and Roberta Smith spoke with Index about Oberhelm's case: "Artists around the world are generally trying to do things that are permissible in democracies but sometimes not in their societies […] Artists must reserve the right to provoke society but that comes with risk and responsibility."

What follows is a selection of emails made available by the Glasgow School of Art.

From: ▮▮▮▮▮▮▮▮▮▮▮▮▮▮▮▮▮▮▮▮
Date: Friday, 7 April 2017 at 14:41
To: ▮▮▮▮▮▮▮▮▮▮▮▮▮▮▮▮▮▮
Cc: ▮▮▮▮▮▮▮▮▮▮▮▮▮▮▮▮
Subject: RE: MFA Interim proposals for review

Hi ▮▮▮▮

I caught up with ▮▮▮ on the phone today about the below as a few of the answers don't provide the info straight off:

As mentioned GSA Exhibitions don't have the contact on electrician details – so if you speak with ▮▮▮▮▮▮ in Estates he is the best person (as ▮▮▮ looks not to know)
Re ▮▮▮▮▮▮▮, I said this may be a project ▮▮ wishes to corresponded as part of the creative act with one of the H&S team – he suggested ▮▮▮▮▮▮. The knife would be classed as a weapon – unless super glued down or in a secure vitrine it could not be loose in the gallery.
Can you forward me the proposal with the explicit video content and its risk assessment that the student has worked on since speaking with you? I will speak with ▮▮▮▮▮▮ first, then it possibly is ▮▮▮▮▮▮ who would sign off on proposed measures brought in to show the piece – you mentioned to ▮▮▮▮ it would be seminar room 2, notice put up etc

▮▮▮▮

From: ▮▮▮▮▮▮▮▮
Sent: 10 April 2017 08:46
To: ▮▮▮▮▮▮▮▮
Cc: ▮▮▮▮▮▮▮▮▮▮
Subject: Re: MFA Interim proposals for review

Hi ▮▮▮

Thanks very much for the further information from ▮▮▮, which was helpful.

I am attaching ▮▮▮▮▮▮▮▮ proposal, Risk Assessment and the link to the youtube film which he will be showing as part of the installation. This film is freely available for anyone to view online. The most difficult imagery takes place in the last 5 minutes of the film.

https://www.youtube.com/watch?v=oy2gHEonz_8

The End of Sykes Picot

www.youtube.com

Disclaimer: Excerpt of jihadist propaganda for educational purpose

What I would add is that ▮▮▮▮ is an excellent student, full of integrity and fully aware of the difficult and potentially distressing nature of the imagery - which he is not treating lightly. He is very alert for the need for it to be dealt with in a sensitive manner and will ensure that as much information as possible is given to audience members prior to entering the space. This will take the form of a sign outside the room, also spoken and written information given to everyone before entering the space. So no one will encounter the work without understanding what it entails and everyone will have a choice about whether to engage with it or not. The plan is for the installation to be in place in the Seminar room on the night of the opening and if possible on a few programmed dates/times during the exhibition run.

We are very supportive of his work and believe it is dealing with important (if difficult) issues at quite a critical time.

If you need any further information, do not hesitate to let us know

▮▮▮▮▮

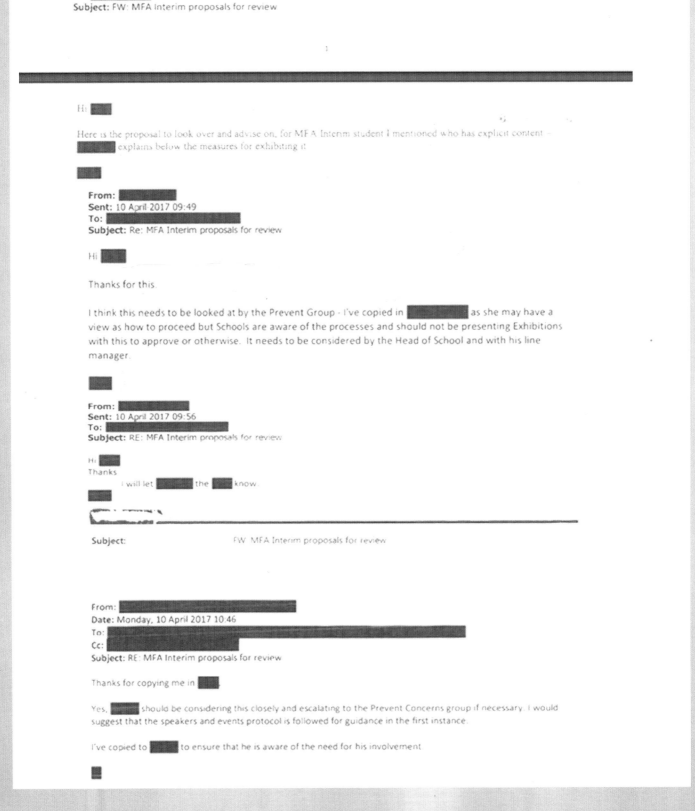

From: ▓▓▓▓▓▓▓▓▓
Sent: 09 April 2017 20:41:22
To: ▓▓▓▓▓▓
Subject: FW: MFA Interim proposals for review

Hi ▓▓

Here is the proposal to look over and advise on, for MFA Interim student I mentioned who has explicit content – ▓▓▓▓ explains below the measures for exhibiting it

▓▓▓

From: ▓▓▓▓▓▓
Sent: 10 April 2017 09:49
To: ▓▓▓▓▓▓▓▓▓▓▓▓
Subject: Re: MFA Interim proposals for review

Hi ▓▓▓

Thanks for this.

I think this needs to be looked at by the Prevent Group - I've copied in ▓▓▓▓▓▓▓ as she may have a view as how to proceed but Schools are aware of the processes and should not be presenting Exhibitions with this to approve or otherwise. It needs to be considered by the Head of School and with his line manager.

▓▓▓

From: ▓▓▓▓▓▓
Sent: 10 April 2017 09:56
To: ▓▓▓▓▓▓▓▓▓
Subject: RE: MFA Interim proposals for review

Hi ▓▓
Thanks
▓▓▓ I will let ▓▓▓▓ the ▓▓ know.
▓▓▓

Subject: FW: MFA Interim proposals for review

From: ▓▓▓▓▓▓▓▓▓▓▓
Date: Monday, 10 April 2017 10:46
To: ▓▓▓▓▓▓▓▓▓▓▓▓▓▓▓
Cc: ▓▓▓▓▓▓▓▓▓
Subject: RE: MFA Interim proposals for review

Thanks for copying me in ▓▓▓.

Yes, ▓▓▓▓ should be considering this closely and escalating to the Prevent Concerns group if necessary. I would suggest that the speakers and events protocol is followed for guidance in the first instance.

I've copied to ▓▓▓▓ to ensure that he is aware of the need for his involvement

▓▓

C. Freedom of Information requests

The internal documents shown above were released following an internal review, requested under Freedom of Information legislation by Nik Williams of Scottish PEN, due to unsatisfactory responses to his earlier requests for an explanation of the censorship decision. All correspondence and documents are in the public domain at:

https://www.whatdotheyknow.com/request/decision_behind_the_removal_of_t#outgoing-648198

Documents are downloadable via links at the bottom of the page.

D. Minutes of meeting on censorship decision, with analytical response by student

Following lengthy correspondence between student James Oberhelm and Student Representative Council Director Laura Glennie, Ms. Glennie held a meeting with GSA Deputy Director (Academic) Prof. Ken Neil, and Head of School of Fine Art Dr. Alastair Payne, to discuss the censorship decision in April made by the GSA Senior Management Team. The minutes were duly forwarded on to the student on that evening:

<u>Laura Glennie to James Oberhelm 28 August 2017</u>

I am writing to you to give updates after meeting with Ken and Alistair, who requested to meet after I mailed them with my concerns (as I told you I had) on 31st of July. We had all been on leave for some consecutive weeks and got together today.

I voiced my concerns about the way this situation was handled and how much support you were given. I had asked for the 'full process' from their point of view. The general consensus still lies that GSA will always 'disallow the public exhibition of murder.'
Here are my notes, copied in full, from the meeting:

"- Alistair praised the fact that all the way through the run up to your show you kept in close contact with Programme Staff about your work.

- The Programme Staff felt uncomfortable with the film part of your show

- The Programme Team brought this concern to the Head of Fine Art, who conversed with Ken Neil (Depute Director, Academic)

- The film part of your show was brought up for discussion at the Senior Management Team Meeting (the timing of which co-incided with these events)

- All 13 members of the SMT decided that showing the film piece was a bad idea and staff were concerned about your welfare in presenting this.

- At this time there was a separate discussion with members of Prevent at GSA and it was decided that this piece would not go to the committee as you obviously did not display signs of being radicalised and that this was more of an academic decision.

- The SMT minute was offered back to you and your Programme Leader would also feed back the SMT decision and talk through the decision. The Programme Leader spoke to you a number of times.

- The Programme Team offered additional support to the you in the coming year.

- The Programme Team expressed that they have no problem with your work or the themes of your work they just wanted to support the welfare of you in this instance.

- Throughout this process, you have always been allowed to present your film work as 'censored' at the MFA Interim Show.

- The school want to continue working with you and hope that you have time to work out what this means."

I really hope that this provided some sort of clarity. Please let me know what you think when you're able to.

<u>Response to minutes by student James Oberhelm and sent to Laura Glennie for the record</u>

1: core criteria for censoring artwork *"Effects" [The Enthronement]* from public exhibition

email reads: The general consensus still lies that GSA will always 'disallow the public exhibition of murder.'

This general principle seems very implausible. Does this mean that the famous film sequence of the execution of Nguyễn Văn Lém in Saigon could not be exhibited? [The sequence was in fact screened on UK national television by the BBC in December 2017, as part of the Ken Burns' documentary series *The Vietnam War,* along with countless other depictions of human death and extreme violence]. The photograph of Sean Downes being shot by a plastic bullet on a Belfast street? Does this extend to images of the terror of the Einsatzgruppen in eastern Europe, or to images of lynching?

As a teenage school pupil studying politics our teacher showed a film which included footage of a Japanese soldier burned to death by flamethrower – impressing on us a reality of war. Could this footage not now be shown in a third-level institution to a public seeking engagement with contemporary fine art? As a gallery technician I worked for some years in Belfast's flagship Ormeau Baths Gallery, where one installation had as its centrepiece the documentary *Executions*, an account of the history of capital punishment. Would staging this work in Glasgow School of Art not be possible?

I have in my possession a photo-illustrated book depicting British imperial India, formerly of Glasgow School of Art library, and sold as remaindered stock shortly after the decision to censor *"Effects" [The Enthronement].* Along with images of splendour, folk-culture, and the genteel rituals of the imperial rulers, are images of execution by firing squad, crucifixion, the skeletal remains of massacred Indian rebels, a mutilated torture victim, severely emaciated peasants during famine, and inhumane treatment of prisoners. This is exactly the type of artefact that serves as direct evidence for understanding and insight – precisely because of its unexpurgated balance between social normality, the façade of power, and the reality of violence and brutality.

In light of the above it remains my view that the key factor in the censoring of *"Effects" [The Enthronement]* is the political content and context of the film element within the work – militant international Jihadism, and the expanding security agenda in the UK and beyond, exemplified by the Prevent directive's intervention in the workings of UK educational institutions, as laid down by the Counter Terrorism and Security Act 2015.

2: secondary matters, addressing the other points covered in the meeting minutes:

Laura I've written previously with a precise account of the sequence of events, so I'll try to be as brief as possible here, while still trying to address the principles involved.

I had open, professional, and thorough discussions with 2 staff members in the course of this – MFA tutors Christina McBride and Sarah Tripp. Both were supportive and critically engaged. Christina communicated to me that they had been cut out of the loop during the screening/evaluation of the piece.

The notes from your meeting give a misleading impression of consultation and openness during the process. There was a long delay in the decision to censor the work being communicated to me, toward the end of which I communicated to Sarah and Christina that the work was effectively being filibustered by the delay. The people/body within the institution that were screening the work did not identify themselves throughout this, and I only became aware that it was in fact the 'Senior Management Team' that had censored the work through a Freedom of Information request made by an independent organization (Scottish PEN).

My meetings with course director Henry Rogers were very brief, and not discussions in any sense: 2 meetings of approximately 5 minutes each, which were effectively bullet-point type exchanges. There was also a very short discussion as part of an MFA 'progress review' meeting between Henry and myself, the day before the censorship decision was communicated, during which Henry asked about my proposed course of action if the work was censored, and I stated that I'd wish to have a display in the exhibition informing visitors that a work had been censored from the show.

I requested to Henry that the criteria for censoring the work be put to me in writing. I made this request twice in writing, and twice in our spoken exchanges. This request was resolutely stonewalled.

The most comprehensive statement remains the cursory one sent to Robert Sharp (of advocacy group English

PEN), by Lesley Booth, of GSA Press and Media department:

> We deemed the filmic material to be inappropriate for public display as we were concerned that the student's use and distribution of that material could present and unacceptable risk for the student and the GSA.

the source of which was given as 'A spokesperson for The Glasgow School of Art'. There was no response to a request for clarification of what was meant by 'unacceptable risk'.

The 'Senior Management Team' minute was not sent to me directly, despite my written and spoken requests, but was released only as part of the Scottish PEN Freedom of Information request, which was made following my being stonewalled. The FOI request was responded to evasively throughout, i.e. the responses tried to 'contain' the matter in terms of the management of the student concerned, rather than clarifying the criteria upon which the artwork had been censored, finally necessitating a request for a full internal Freedom of Information review for release of any relevant documents. It is in this context that verbiage of institutional 'support' was made – evasive responses to an outside advocate's request for transparency and clarity on the issue of censorship of artwork from public exhibition.

The manner and intent of such proposed 'support' itself raises important questions. For example the SRC minute released as part of the Freedom of Information exchange read:

> The group decided that this particular film should not be shown and that the student be supported in moving forward in terms of professional practice and understanding the implications of their work including the presentation of online sources.

which prompted one third-sector advocate, who was monitoring the situation, to comment that he was "quite alarmed that self-censorship is implied here, as part of teaching artists professional practice/development."

In my communications with MFA programme leader/course director Henry Rogers I made it clear that, in the important matter of the censorship of artwork from public exhibition, the minimum requirement for institutional transparency was that the basis for the decision be given to me directly in writing. The choice to task the programme leader/course director as messenger-spokesperson for the SMT in the matter of artistic censorship, in the absence of transparent communications (i.e. direct, relevant, clear, and comprehensive, written communications), indicated a failure to protect the integrity of the course director-student relationship; to all appearances the priority seemed to be that institutional containment, and avoiding a paper-trail, were the top priority, to the detriment of staff-student working relations in the MFA department. When I tried to redress this, by asking (in writing to Henry) whom I should address further enquiries to, so that I wouldn't have to go through MFA staff, I was ignored. An incident of public dispute between the course director and myself, during an MFA group crit, which occurred in the presence of several witnesses, and which I have recorded in notes written up shortly afterwards, made this compromising of the course director's role particularly evident. Such are the circumstances that arise when transparency is lacking.

It is not in any way established that 'supporting welfare' is a sound basis for artistic censorship in this case. The issue of welfare within professional life, for staff and students alike, is important in its own right. It is ill-served when used as a rhetorical convenience in the case for censorship. This raises the question of how the verbiage of support and welfare may be being utilized in this instance as "a verbal shield against accountability". Journalist Fintan O'Toole uses this term to describe the institutional use of lexical obfuscation as a strategy to manage politically uncomfortable circumstances; following on from bluntly ignoring requests for written clarification, the written responses to freedom of information requests resemble an attempt to create just such a shield against accountability.

Finally – regarding mention of the issue of 'radicalization', even a brief review in the field raises questions about the interpretation of Prevent in a way that causes a 'chilling effect' on debate, for example in the work of Prof. Paul Thomas, and David Anderson QC. The latter comments:

> this culture of silence is the opposite to what is intended in the government's Prevent Duty guidelines, which state that schools should make it easy for young people to discuss sensitive topics

(which of course isn't to accept that the principle of the prevent directive is sound in the first instance, regardless of how it is interpreted, or implemented; this being a matter of much ongoing debate.)w

16

E. Report for Artist Rights Justice Working Group, and UN Special Rapporteur on cultural rights, sent October 2017

Required information for cases sent to the UN Special Rapporteur on cultural rights

Artistic freedom

1. **When and Where**. Date, time and precise location of the incident (country, region, municipality, area).

If applicable indicate whether it is a public or private space (i.e. gallery, museum, theatre, street, cinema, etc)

Glasgow School of Art, Glasgow, Scotland

2. **What happened**. Detailed circumstances of the alleged violation. If an initial event leads to others, describe them chronologically.

In case of general measures such as national legislation or policies, indicate their stage of development and how artists and cultural actors have or will be affected by them.

    a)   Date: April / May 2017 – The interim show the piece was intended to be screened at took place on the 5th May 2017 as part of the exhibition launch.
    b)   Place: Glasgow School of Art
    c)   Time: n/a

INFORMATION REGARDING THE ALLEGED VIOLATION

    d)   The nature of the incident: Describe the circumstances of the incident:

James Oberhelm is a Fine Art student at the Glasgow School of Art and as part of his course he developed a multimedia art project for the school's interim show that ran between 6th and 13th May 2017, entitled "Effects" [The Enthronement]. The piece was "an installation dealing with the geopolitics of the Middle East. It is timed to coincide with the centenary of the 1914-18 war, and the redrawing of borders that occurred at that time. It specifically addresses the 1916 Sykes-Picot agreement, a secret agreement between Britain and France (with the complicity of Russia) to redraw the map of the Middle East. This agreement shot to public awareness when ISIS released a propaganda video in 2014 titled 'The End of Sykes Picot', following the organization's capture of territories stretching across Syria and Iraq."

As part of the installation, the piece proposed playing two films (total run time 27m 15s), issued by Al-Hayat in 2014. These films are publicly available on YouTube but show difficult imagery related to executions carried out by ISIS militants. In the process of putting together the installation, Oberhelm completed a risk assessment and established a range of steps to ensure potential viewers were aware of the complex and challenging content. This included the involvement of two staff members including a security guard outside and an invigilator/consultant inside. There would also be clearly visible sign outside the room warning viewers that the installation will contain graphic and potentially disturbing content, which would also be contained in all written materials provided in the exhibition.

Following an FOI internal review called for by Scottish PEN, internal emails revealed that on 10th April an unnamed GSA staff member stated that the piece should be escalated "to the Prevent Concerns group if necessary". This was reiterated in an email to James Oberhelm on 11th April. Following this exchange, Oberhelm was informed that of the three pieces that forming his part of the show, the piece with the film footage was removed from the show. It is important to state that the artist was informed as a result of a chance meeting with the MFA course director Henry Rogers and he hasn't received a formal written statement as to the censoring of his work. He was also promised the minutes of working meeting where the decision was made to remove his piece. He is yet to receive this.

3. **Victim(s)**. Name, number and full details about the artist, cultural center or other concerned actor that has been or is at risk as result of alleged fact.

James Oberhelm

4. **Perpetrator(s)**. Information on who allegedly committed the violation. If known, an explanation of the reasons why they are suspected of being responsible.

Glasgow School of Art

5. **Action taken by national authorities** : when the authorities are not the perpetrator, has the matter been reported to the national administrative or judicial authorities? If applicable, what actions have been taken by the relevant authorities to remedy the situation?

n/a

6. **Action taken by other actors** : Has any legal action been initiated before international or regional human rights mechanisms? What is the state of development of these actions?

Using the Freedom of Information Act, Scottish PEN requested all "correspondence, information or documents held by the GSA regarding the decision to remove the piece...as well as the grounds for its removal." Due to the lack of information shared within the designated time frame as outlined by the FOI Act, Scottish PEN requested an internal review which secured a number of emails, as well as the risk assessment process outlined by the GSA.

Index on Censorship covered the story, including the information received through FOI requests here, here and here.

7. **Source**: Name and full address of the organization or individual(s) submitting the information. The details about the person or the organization submitting the information is essential in case that the Rapporteur would need clarification or further information on the case. This information is always kept confidential.

Here we have to include information about ARJ as the organization submitting the information but also the information about the original source and who to contact to know more and follow up on the case. « The information concerning this case was transmitted by X organization that can be contacted for more information (give contact details) »

« ARJ has leant for X,Y,Z organization, newsletter, etc that... »

Organisation name: Scottish PEN
Contact: Acting-Project Manager, Nicholas Williams
Email: nik@scottishpen.org

Remember: there is only one person at the UN receiving all the information. You should prepare the case to the extent possible so he/she only has to double-check the information. Over time when ARJ becomes a fully entrusted case provider, they will consider information coming from us is reliable which entails a responsibility to check our sources.

7. Action requested

Here you can specify what type of action is needed: in general a letter to the authorities. At the end of the year, when the Special Rapporteur presents its report and actions, all cases will be included.

Contact information

Information addressed to the Special Rapporteur should be sent by mail, fax or e-mail to:

Special Rapporteur in the field of cultural rights
Office of the High Commissioner for Human Rights United Nations c/o OHCHR-UNOG CH-1211 Geneva 10

SwitzerlandFax: (+41 22) 917 90 06

E-mail: urgent-action@ohchr.org srculturalrights@ohchr.org

Twitter: @UNSRCulture

F. 'The "Effects" of Censorship'

Paul Aitken

First published in Art Review Glasgow, November 2017. available at:

http://artreviewglasgow.org/the-effects-of-censorship

The richly industrious nature of the city of Glasgow has allowed it to develop a high-end artistic scene as well as a distinctively straightforward and forthcoming character. It seems to have been able to retain and develop a certain social and political sovereignty, and is renowned for its people and gregariousness. This, in particular, is why it seems like such a shame that Glasgow School of Art has – for the first time in its history – censored the work of a student from exhibition. A piece entitled *"Effects"* - from a wider work called *The Enthronement* by James Oberhelm of the Masters of Fine Art (MFA) – was concerned with our cultures wars - past and present. It commented on and provided means for considering these conflicts from within and outwith the common perspective. It would have been, in my estimation, a particularly stark but engaging piece; difficult to ignore and easy to understand. It was due to be shown at the MFA interim exhibition in May, but the Senior Management Team (SMT) decided to censor it in unanimity.

Although two other pieces of *The Enthronement* were displayed the proposed exhibition space for *"Effects"* contained instead an open book entitled *The Shock of The New*, a poster quoting material from the Records Office active during the 1914-1918 war and some pamphlets explaining that *"Effects"* was censored, with a list of the materials that would have been used. These are thus: a replica of "Army Form B. 101-82"; the official notification letter sent to next of kin in the event of a soldier's death during the first world war. There was to be the type of typewriter, and a desk and chair from that period. There would have been a laptop linked to UK Ministry of Defence Joint Casualty and Compassionate Centre website - which offers support and guidance to the next of kin of those who die in military service, there would have been a modern desk and chair by that. There would be a replica of the Sykes-Picot Agreement map, a map depicting initial secret arrangements between Britain and France for division of much of the Middle East into spheres of imperial influence from 1916. We would find a video projection of *The End of Sykes Picot*, and *Kaser al-Hudud (the breaking of the borders)* - propaganda videos issued by Al Hayat, the media outlet for Daesh/ISIS from 29 June 2014 – these videos included executions. There would have been booklets containing historical-political contextual materials relating to Sykes-Picot Agreement and Daesh/ISIS published between 2015 and 2016 by political analysts. The rest of the materials I quote: "contemporary stretch barrier; a security guard; a printed sign reading 'contains graphic and potentially disturbing content'; some printed leaflets containing descriptive guidance for the work and further notification as to the potential distress caused by its content and finally a staff member available for instruction as to structure and duration of the installation, and for discussion and assistance upon request by attendees." The highly controversial nature of the sorts of materials displayed are probably evident, but did it deserve to be censored? What is behind the censorship? Should we put our foot down? And if not, when?

I met the artist in the Savoy Centre, near GSA, to talk about the issues at hand. The censorship is – as far as Oberhelm is concerned – politically motivated. "Prevent is at the heart of this", I'm told. The Prevent Strategy is a government campaign aimed at stopping radicalisation in educational institutions, it has been active in its present capacity in Scotland since 2015. There is a Prevent Concerns Group (PCG) in all educational institutions, at GSA, there are seventeen members, including the director, the deputy director and the head of the school of fine art. *"Effects"* was never actually formally referred to the PCG, so why does the artist believe that Prevent was at the core of the decision?

Dr Rizwaan Sabir – who was himself arrested under Prevent whilst studying towards his masters - suggests that a lot of misrepresentation of information and buck-passing between police, Prevent members and institutions is endemic in cases such as these. He said that Prevent "attempts to silence, and does silence dissent and resistance. it seeks to instil a form of self-discipline because it's ultimately based on a potential of force being used".

Nik Williams – who works with Scottish PEN – has submitted two Freedom of Information requests with regards this case, leading to the disclosure of notes from meetings, the forms submitted for the installation and some e-mails between GSA faculty. Williams asked for "all information related to the schools Prevent Concerns Group" and was told that "since the case was never referred to Prevent, No Prevent related concern has been referred for consideration: the subgroup has therefore never been convened." This is despite minutes of a meeting between departmental heads and the Director of the Students Representatives Council (SCR), in which the Director of the SRC wrote to the artist "there was a separate discussion with members of Prevent at GSA and it was decided that this piece would not go to the committee as you obviously did not display signs of being radicalised and that this was more of an academic decision."

Maybe it was an academic decision, and Oberhelm is a rubbish artist, full of baloney. But, in an e-mail sent by a faculty member containing the execution video for review, they write, "What I would add is that James is an excellent student, full of integrity and fully aware of the potentially distressing nature of the imagery – which he is not treating lightly". The plea for consideration continues for a number of sentences, ending with "We are very supporting of his work and believe it is dealing with important (if difficult) issues at quite a critical time". The decision to censor was unanimous amongst seventeen members of the SMT. There's something amiss here, given the fact that Oberhelm's approach and work are regarded highly within the institution.

Because the PCG never convened, there is no available information. But it doesn't seem likely that such a group might ever need to "convene" formally in order to make decisions. One can only speculate at this stage how many overlapping members of the SMT and the PCG there are. Prevent needn't be involved if the school simply censors the offending article, as appears to have happened here. Prevent is obviously deeply rooted in the school – as it must be in many institutions. Were it not for the pressures of Prevent, the work may not have been censored.

The wording of the revised Prevent Duty Guidance for Scotland (2015) specifically refers to "Islamist extremists", "The white supremacist ideology" and "The threat from terrorism relating to Northern Ireland" - in which there are "several dissident republican groups". According to the guidelines, "The Government has defined extremism under the Prevent Strategy as: "vocal or active opposition to fundamental British values, including democracy, the rule of law, individual liberty and mutual respect and tolerance of different faiths and beliefs". There is a group operating by assimilations of these values nested in our educational institutions. It seems to me concerning, particularly when the policy has the full weight of the law behind it. The idea that you cannot question the rule of law or someone else's faiths and beliefs is written into the law.

This article does not seek to single out, defend or speak for the artist or the institution in question, but to comment on the culture within which they operate. Dr Sabir argues that it is often "incompetence over conspiracy" that results in the mishandling of cases where Prevent is involved, so whether it is a culture of incompetence or a culture of conspiracy, that culture is important. Michael Attenborough has commented on the threat to artistic culture presented by the "catastrophe" of "self-censorship" that is "creeping in" to exhibitions for the last few years. *"Effects"* was censored, and the new first year MFA students have been told in no uncertain terms that the GSA will not exhibit certain materials, with specific reference made regarding terrorism – undoubtedly a response to the "Effects" case. These two steps make way down a very dark path as far as I can tell.

Despite the institutions best efforts, *"Effects"* is still in motion. This article is testament to that – perhaps it would have been wiser for them to simply exhibit the material, since it doesn't look as if the problem is going away. It is important to stand up against censorship; Oberhelm tells me that – as an artist – this is less about moral courage and more about professional responsibility. When we accept censorship, we have sacrificed freedom of expression. This sacrifice should not, and must not, stand.

SECTION IV: SUMMARY ESSAY

Glasgow School of Art: case study in The New Censorship

Om Lekha

Since early 2017 Glasgow School of Art, an art school associated with high-profile experimental art practice in the UK, has steadily emerged as a case study in the new forms of censorship seeking to curtail expression and discussion in the academic environment. The school's actions centre on the previously well-regarded Master of Fine Art Programme.

Beginning in April of 2017 the school censored a political artwork from public exhibition, the first time in the history of the course. The art installation, *"Effects" [The Enthronement]*, was scheduled for exhibition in the Glasgow School of Art's 'Interim Show' in May 2017. The installation would have addressed the geopolitics of the Middle East region over the past century, and the intimate impact of war due to bereavement. It would have presented the various forms of media and technology used during that time, by imperialist and fundamentalist organizations, and by bureaucracies trying to cope with the realities of casualties incurred by military service.

In representing the trajectory from the geopolitics of the 1914-18 war to the conflicts of today the installation included two videos issued in 2014 by Al-Hayat, the media outlet of Daesh/ISIS. The videos in question address the Sykes-Picot Agreement of 1916, out of which the current Iraq-Syria border was initially conceived. They were to be counterposed in the artwork by the 1916 map depicting the first proposed border. The decision to censor focused on the inclusion of the contemporary videos, to the exclusion of all other aspects of the work.

In previous cases where artworks proposed for exhibition contained difficult or distressing content, this was addressed through a consultative process, and an appropriate management plan for exhibition of the artwork. Despite a similar process in this case the artwork was censored on the grounds of 'inappropriate content'. As previous artworks have also included difficult material, yet gone ahead to exhibition, it was clear that the censorship of this piece had a political dimension. The artistic employment and context of the videos, which located them as part of the semiotics of control, intersecting with lived reality across the historical timespan, was discounted. Other concerns took precedence.

A later statement made by the school's Head of Fine Art, and Deputy Director, professed the grounds for censorship as "The general consensus still lies that GSA will always 'disallow the public exhibition of murder.'", which fails to accord with a huge amount of precedent in the arts and in culture more broadly (in fact shortly after the censorship occurred the BBC screened on UK national television the infamous film-sequence of Vietcong Nguyễn Văn Lém being executed on a Saigon street).

It was clear that the key factor in censoring the artwork was the political content and context of the film element within the work – militant international Jihadism, and the expanding security agenda in the UK and beyond, exemplified by the UK government Prevent Duty's intervention in the workings of UK educational institutions, as laid down by the *Counter Terrorism and Security Act 2015*. The Prevent directive requires UK education institutions to monitor students and pupils for signs of political radicalization, and remains hotly contested by many in the education sector, and across society.

Like other education institutions in the UK Glasgow School of Art has a formally constituted 'Prevent Group', set up under the terms of the *Counter Terrorism and Security Act 2015*. Members of this group may well have been involved in the decision to censor, as many of the same staff sit on the Senior Management Team, who took the formal decision to censor the work. One journalist writing on the affair has noted that:

> Because the PCG [Prevent Concerns Group] never convened, there is no available information. But it doesn't seem likely that such a group might ever need to "convene" formally in order to make decisions. One can only speculate at this stage how many overlapping members of the SMT and the PCG there are. Prevent needn't be involved if the school simply censors the offending article, as appears to have happened here. Prevent is obviously deeply rooted in the school – as it must be in many institutions. Were it not for the pressures of Prevent, the work may not have been censored.

Of much greater significance, the censorship of this artwork has not remained a potentially one-off event, but segued into a new policy and direction at the art school. At a formal induction in September 2017 the recently appointed MFA Programme Leader issued incoming students with a warning that artwork they produce for exhibition will be subject to limits determined by the school, specifically citing work which includes 'terrorist materials' as an example. The culmination came in November 2017, with a newly created MFA Handbook, which massively expands the terms of potential future censorship, making clear to all students that they must produce work that is considered acceptable.

The Handbook sections which aim at curtailing free-expression, encouraging self-censorship, and ideological conformity, are presented under the banners of 'ethos' and 'ethics'. They demonstrate the 'sophisticated censor's' method of shutting-down opposing views; using rhetoric around cultural sensitivity, and the demand for sophisticated communication, in order to extend and maintain the practice of censorship under extremely broad and interpretable terms: work that is deemed insensitive, ethically irresponsible, offensive, inappropriate, or disreputable.

Work dealing with sexuality, religion, death, and sociopolitical conflict could all easily fall under the definition of what could be considered unacceptable, or disreputable, by the school. The first three categories are indicated as 'sensitive' areas by the school's postgraduate ethics policy document, which also repeatedly cites the contested 'Prevent duty'.

Current trends towards the suppression of free expression and open discussion in higher education are well recognized. These raise complex and contested issues, often centred on explicit practices such as no-platforming and safe-space policies, but which are also maintained by the pervading public culture of an institution (which speakers are invited, what topics are foregrounded, what frames of reference are used when introducing those topics, what texts are cited and set, what public events are hosted, what exhibitions and events are supported, what aesthetic forms are visible, etc. – and crucially then what is not addressed or articulated as a result) that standardize what is 'acceptable' in that environment.

Artists, and the humanities-educated milieu more widely (who are overwhelmingly self-identified as 'progressive'), are particularly cowed by the spectre of 'hate speech', when it is suggested that they will become guilty by association if they fail to comply with new forms of censorship and self-censorship. In effect they have become complicit in an ideological drift whereby a social justice agenda has been allowed (or encouraged) to separate from basic principles of liberty, thus gifting their political enemies the opportunity to claim these principles as their own. In the short term this is proving ineffective, as political developments show, and in the medium to long term it's unlikely to promote the vitality of human creativity.

All artists, and all people, must navigate the social norms that hold sway in their milieu, if they are to achieve deeper, more honest, and more accurate communications with others. Glasgow School of Art has made itself noteworthy by elevating these norms from pervasive and implicit prohibitions into explicit policies and directives delivered direct to students, and by issuing an open declaration of what constitutes acceptable ideology and ways of communicating. That it does so in the field of artistic expression, which has often remained an area where oppressive and constricting orthodoxies can be played with, examined, and eluded, is of particular concern.

The net intent is clear, the design to exclude difficult ideas, and forms of expression, and to suppress unacceptable views; in other words to engineer a climate of opinion, rather than develop knowledge.

So, there is a two-tiered erosion of open expression underway within education, culture, and the arts: the time-honoured prohibitions of the 'security agenda', as imposed by the political establishment, and the programme of hip new overseers to engineer ongoing self-censorship by emergent artists according to prescriptive norms and values. The latter is more insidious, because it undermines free thinking and open expression closer to the root, and less as a symptom. Like the Jesuits of old it aims to mould thought at its inception, not merely get people to fall into line.

Glasgow School of Art serves as a neat case-study in how these trends are evolving, and inter-relating, in recent times.

https://www.indexoncensorship.org/2017/05/glasgow-school-of-art-censorship-isis/

the voice of free expression

NEWS

Students at Glasgow School of Art fight programme-sanctioned censorship

13 Apr 2018
BY RYAN MCCHRYSTAL

Glasgow School of Art. Credit: James Oberhelm

After the Glasgow School of Art censored an artwork by master of fine art student James Oberhelm from a May 2017 interim show when it was deemed to contain "inappropriate content", the commitment of the world-famous institution to free speech has again come into question. Students enrolled in the programme were issued an updated handbook in November 2017 with provisions that would make such censorship much more likely and much easier to enforce in future.

These were without precedent, urging students to exercise caution when it comes to "offensive" or "inappropriate" material and warning against "bringing the institution into disrepute". It goes on to say that the "right to freedom of speech is not absolute", requiring students to adhere to the "highest ethical standards" and "ethical good practice".

Over two-thirds of MFA students at the school have signed a petition calling for such rules to be removed and demanding an environment where they can work "free from the threat of being banned by GSA." "Censorship is fundamentally a point of principle, even if it doesn't affect an individual practice right now," it adds.

Oberhelm is one of the 34 out of a total of 50 MFA students who have signed the recent petition. His artwork, "Effects" [The Enthronement], explored the geopolitics of the Middle East and included a propaganda video created by Isis. An email between staff members at the internationally famous art school stated that Oberhelm's "needs to be looked at by the Prevent Group", referring to the UK's counterterrorism legislation Prevent. Past and present staff at the world-famous institution have confirmed to Oberhelm that this was the first case of censorship in its history.

"It's self-evident that open expression is fundamental to creative work and study," he told Index. "The threat of censorship undermines open expression and the attempt to engender self-censorship is corrupting to art practice and to art education. Art is a space of potential and a discipline of vital exchange, not a tool for social engineering and ideological conformity."

Henry Rogers, MFA programme leader at the school, replied to the signatories of the petition with the following [sic]: "we have as a team discussed petition about the ethical practice advisory statements in the MFA Handbook that some people have signed. Of course we are happy to look at this when preparing the 2018-2019 Handbook (normally a summer task for staff) and will consult you again at that point once the handbook has been revised. If there are any other amendment you feel you want to bring to the fore, please do let me know."

"The MFA programme leader's response is unsatisfactory in that it has simply delayed the decision until after this academic year ends, thus ensuring that an entire year of students, who have become well-informed about GSA's advancing censorship practices, will be gone when a decision is made," Oberhelm said. "While this delay of many months might come dressed in a procedural rationale, it also looks very much like the time-honoured institutional strategy of drawing out the process till the opposition dissipates."

But Oberhelm remains hopeful that the Glasgow School of Art "still has the wherewithal to defend its reputation by removing these written directives, and ceasing the practice of briefing incoming postgrad students to police their art practice, rather than allow its reputation to become steadily more tarnished".

w

Below is a list of works that likely wouldn't be acceptable forms of expression under the Glasgow School of Art's new rules and provisions:

SECTION VI: QUESTIONS REGARDING GSA STAFF CONDUCT

A list of initial questions on procedure and professional conduct regarding the matters covered in this publication are listed below. They are the basic general questions that arise for a non-specialist in law, policy and governance matters, and do not claim to be otherwise. The author did benefit from consultation with a professional with specialist knowledge in the area (ethics, policy, and governance in UK third-level arts education), speaking off the record, but the questions are independently drafted by the author.

If the stated reasons for censorship in April 2017 do not stand up to scrutiny (1 disallow the public exhibition of murder 2 protect well-being of student), what is the actual reason, or reasons, for censorship, including the possibility that consideration of the Prevent Duty was integral to the decision to censor?

What is the shared personnel of the Senior Management Team and the Prevent Group at Glasgow School of Art?

Why did GSA refuse to provide in writing the reasons for the censorship in April 2017, despite requests by the student concerned, and why did the MFA Programme Leader facilitate GSA avoiding a paper-trail regarding this censorship by acting as spokesperson for the SMT, despite the fact that he is not a member of the SMT?

Do any questions regarding professional conduct arise, due to the MFA Programme Leader's acquiescence to becoming spokesperson for the SMT, as this pertains to the compromising of the staff-student relationship (by acting as advocate for the SMT position, to the detriment of his role as advocate for the interests of the MFA student-body)?

Did the MFA Programme Leader's public behaviour provide supporting evidence for the latter point above, when publicly characterizing the censored student's response as 'escalating the situation' at a group crit (11th May 2017), in front of another staff member and six students, thereby signalling to the student group that a student who questions their work being censored, requests a written explanation for this, and draws public attention to censorship, will be 'marked-out' for doing so?

Do procedural questions arise from the above with regards to the MFA Programme Leader's ability to act impartially with regards to students, potentially prejudicing his role as assessor of students' work and academic output while on the course. i.e. if students feel that the Programme Leader is acting on behalf of the interests of GSA management, and is not impartial when students object to actions taken by the management which are to the detriment of student interests, then students may be inhibited in 'speaking out' if this brings them into conflict with a member of staff who can affect the marks that they eventually get, and who is furthermore in a position to provide academic references, facilitate professional connections etc.? In short: does the handling of the censorship in April-May 2017, and actions to impose a censorship agenda in September and November of that year, evidence a professional error of judgement as to his actual responsibilities as a Programme Leader – to support the MFA Programme, rather than to impose a management agenda to the detriment of the MFA Programme?

Could GSA's refusal to supply written reasons for censorship in April 2017, and subsequent evasions of questions sent by Nik Williams of Scottish PEN, resulting in his calling for a full internal review to release documents on the matter, be fairly interpreted as an attempt to obfuscate and contain, i.e. cover-up, their decision? Furthermore, if consideration of the Prevent Duty was integral to the decision to censor the work, could this covering-up be fairly described as having a political dimension?

What is the MFA Programme Leader's account of what he said to incoming MFA Year 1 students in Sept 2017, regarding limitations that could be set on their work? Was his statement composed on his own initiative, or in consultation with/under instruction by other staff or bodies in the institution? On what basis does the MFA Programme Leader claim authority to issue a warning of potential censorship to incoming students, and is this claimed authority in accordance with UK and international law?

If it is not in accordance with the law, do further issues around professional conduct arise from this initiative to threaten censorship, and foster self-censorship, on a postgraduate art programme, either on the part of the MFA Programme Leader if it was his sole initiative, or a collection of staff if it was not his sole initiative?

Was the 'Ethical Good Practice' section of the Handbook written on the sole initiative of the MFA Programme Leader, or in consultation with, or under instruction by, other staff members at GSA? Is it in fact lawful to issue such a censorship warning in writing to postgraduate art students regarding the work they may produce?

Is there a professional irregularity in the use of 'ethics' in the MFA Programme Handbook, when its usual application is to pure research, rather than artistic output, and then to address specific identifiable issues, such as data protection, and working with vulnerable people? Is there any question of procedural 'abuse of ethics and governance' (as one off-the-record advisor on the matter put it to the author), and therefore grounds for calling into question the professional judgment of the MFA Programme Leader, and any other parties he may have been professionally advised or instructed by, given the seriousness of the issue of censorship in the arts, and in the educational environment?

Is this potential abuse of procedure compounded and furthered by setting out the relationship of educator to student as hierarchically coercive, for example in describing the educator's role as one of 'inculcating' prescribed values, discourses and behaviours, and by stating that students must accept limits of expression enforced on them by the institution as the price for access to facilities, and resources?

Why was the Handbook drafted without consultation with the MFA students?

Were the MFA staff aware of, and consulted on, the censorious directives in the new Handbook?

Why was at least one MFA staff member unaware of the censorship directives in the Handbook even after its having been sent to students, and only learned of them from a student by way of an incidental meeting in a corridor (28th November 2017)? Does this ignorance of the development of censorship directives issued to the students through the Handbook, and at the induction of the incoming student year-group, apply to the other MFA staff members?

a thousand complexities of thought
and sentiment, overcome at last (on
both sides) by the hideousness of their
fate, in which they were victims,
and revolting against that mutual,
unceasing massacre, by a rising from
the trenches with a shout of

"We're all fools! . . . Let's all go home!"

– Phillip Gibbs, *Realities of War*, 1920

First Published 2018 by Ichor Inc. Agency

Edited by Om Lekha

ISBN 978-0-9935563-1-9

ISBN 978-0-9935563-1-9

9 780993 556319